Cause and Effect

Reading Comprehension Book
Reading Level 2.0–3.5

Introduction

Welcome to the Edupress Cause and Effect Reading Comprehension Book. This resource is an effective tool for instruction, practice, and evaluation of student understanding. It includes ideas on how to introduce cause and effect to students, as well as activities to help teach and practice the concept.

The reproducible activities in this book are tailored to individual, small-group, and whole-class work. They include leveled reading passages, graphic organizers, worksheets, and detailed instruction pages. These activities provide opportunities to use text, illustrations, graphics, and combinations of these elements to identify cause-and-effect relationships.

The material in this book is written for readers at the 2.0–3.5 reading level. However, the activities can easily be adapted to your students' ability levels and your time frame. After introducing an activity to students, model it by working through one or two examples aloud. You may wish to also read text passages aloud to students, or they can be read silently or aloud by students. For students who need personalized help, individual and small-group activities have been included. These activities can be done alone or with a classroom aide for explicit instruction.

We know you will be pleased with the progress your students make in understanding cause and effect after using this book.

ISBN 13: 978-1-56472-152-5

www.edupressinc.com

Table of Contents

Directions: Cause and Effect Match-Up

Whole Class 

Introduce the idea of reading for cause and effect. Read a short picture book, such as *The Wind Blew* by Pat Hutchins. On a card or sentence strip, write, "The wind blew." Ask students what happens in the story when the wind blows. On a card, write, "It took Mr. White's umbrella." Explain that the first sentence was the cause, and the second sentence was the effect. Then, ask what happens at the end of the story when the wind changes its mind.

Explain that the class will be matching Cause and Effect Cards. Display example cards: "I stayed out in the rain. I got wet."; "I dropped my pencil. I leaned over to pick it up." Remind students that the cause happens first, and the effect happens as a result of the cause. Divide the class into two teams. Reproduce a set of Cause and Effect Cards on page 4 for each team, and cut them apart. Review that a cause begins the process and an event follows. Have one team read aloud a Cause Card. Students on both teams should search their Effect Cards for an appropriate match. The first team to find a correct match and read it aloud wins a point. Does the group agree it is a logical match? Repeat as time allows.

Individual ●

Reproduce several sets of Cause and Effect Cards, and cut them apart. Give each student three or four pairs of cards that are mixed up. Ask them to match the pairs. Have students read their finished pairs aloud to you, or provide them with an answer key to self-check.

Small Group 

Divide the class into small groups. Reproduce the Cause and Effect Cards for each group, cut them apart, and mix them up. Lay the cards facedown on a desk. Explain the game of concentration. Students will take turns turning over two cards. If the students think the cards are a match, the student reads the pair aloud and the group decides whether the pair is accurate. If the cards are correct, the student keeps them. Play continues to the left. Continue until one student has three matches and wins the game.

Answer Key

Cause and Effect Cards (page 4)

Ⓒ It started to rain. Ⓔ Bob opened his umbrella.

Ⓒ The frightened bird flew away quickly.
Ⓔ A colorful feather drifted down.

Ⓒ Jill was hungry. Ⓔ She ate an apple.

Ⓒ Grandpa needs a partner to play checkers.
Ⓔ He will teach Dillon how to play.

Ⓒ Amber saw a jellyfish.
Ⓔ She called her mother to look at the creature.

Ⓒ The worker wants to fix the roof.
Ⓔ He puts a ladder against the building.

Ⓒ Adam pushed the button.
Ⓔ The elevator began to move.

Ⓒ Ellie found a gift for Dad.
Ⓔ She gave her money to the clerk.

Ⓒ The weather was getting warmer.
Ⓔ Tulips began to appear.

Ⓒ Emma saw her mistake. Ⓔ She erased her answer.

Ⓒ It was not time for the parade.
Ⓔ The people sat and waited.

Ⓒ Zack blew a bubble. Ⓔ It floated in the air.

Ⓒ The bees gathered pollen.
Ⓔ They carried it to the hive.

Ⓒ The artist saw a beautiful flower.
Ⓔ She wanted to paint it.

Ⓒ A caterpillar makes a cocoon.
Ⓔ Soon a butterfly comes out.

Ⓒ The farmer wanted to plant vegetables.
Ⓔ He used a hoe to break up the dirt.

Cause and Effect Cards

C It started to rain.	Bob opened his umbrella. E
C The frightened bird flew away quickly.	A colorful feather drifted down. E
C Jill was hungry.	She ate an apple. E
C Grandpa needs a partner to play checkers.	He will teach Dillon how to play. E
C Amber saw a jellyfish.	She called her mother to look at the creature. E
C The worker wants to fix the roof.	He puts a ladder against the building. E
C Adam pushed the button.	The elevator began to move. E
C Ellie found a gift for Dad.	She gave her money to the clerk. E
C The weather was getting warmer.	Tulips began to appear. E
C Emma saw her mistake.	She erased her answer. E
C It was not time for the parade.	The people sat and waited. E
C Zack blew a bubble.	It floated in the air. E
C The bees gathered pollen.	They carried it to the hive. E
C The artist saw a beautiful flower.	She wanted to paint it. E
C A caterpillar makes a cocoon.	Soon a butterfly comes out. E
C The farmer wanted to plant vegetables.	He used a hoe to break up the dirt. E

Directions: Historical Cause and Effect

Whole Class ●●●

Reproduce "A New Country" or "Learning about History" on page 6 or 7 for each student as well as on transparencies. Have students volunteer to read paragraphs out loud. Then, ask students to find as many cause-and-effect pairings in the story as they can. Underline the cause and circle the corresponding effect on the transparency of the story. Then, complete the graphic organizer transparency as a class, writing the causes in the left column and the effects in the right column. Explain that asking, "Why did this happen?" and "What was the result?" can help determine cause and effect. Also explain that a cause can have more than one effect.

Individual ●

Reproduce "A New Country" or "Learning about History" and the graphic organizer for each student. Explain to students that they will read the passage and fill in the "Why" and "What" columns on the graphic organizer. Students who struggle with cause and effect will benefit from using this question strategy.

Small Group ●●

Divide students into pairs. Reproduce one of the stories for both students, as well as one graphic organizer per pair. Explain that the pairs will read the passage together, taking turns reading the paragraphs out loud.

Then, using the graphic organizer, one student will fill in the cause (why) statements, and the other student will fill in the effect (what) statements. After completing the sheet, the students should check their answers to make sure they answer "Why?" and "What?" for each cause and effect.

Answer Key (suggested answers)

"A New Country" (Page 6)

C: You will miss your old friends.
E: You are sad to leave.

C: You pack your things.
E: They will get to your new home safely.

C: You see new places. E: You are excited.

C: People wanted to live in the New World.
E: They decided to leave.

C: Pilgrims had a different religion.
E: The English government treated them badly.

C: Pilgrims wanted freedom.
E: They decided they would have to leave England.

C: Pilgrims did not know much about the New World.
E: They were nervous.

C: Pilgrims needed a lot of food. E: They went hunting, picked berries and nuts, and planted corn.

C: Native Americans had lived in the New World for a long time. E: They knew all about the foods.

C: Native Americans helped the Pilgrims.
E: The Pilgrims were grateful.

C: People wanted to see new places, find good jobs, or didn't like their old homes. E: They moved.

C: Many people moved to the New World.
E: They made a new country, the United States.

"Learning About History" (Page 7)

C: You look at your baby book.
E: You see your own history.

C: The person who took care of you wrote in your book.
E: You can read about important moments in your life.

C: Someone wrote about things that happened.
E: We know about people from long ago.

C: Someone painted pictures.
E: We know what the world looked like back then.

C: People put stories and pictures in history books.
E: We can pick up a book and learn about the past.

C: Someone saved your hair. E: You can see and feel it.

C: Someone saved your birthday card.
E: You can look at the signature.

C: A museum is open to the public.
E: Every person can go and see old objects.

C: Teachers want kids to see things they've read about in history books. E: They take students on field trips.

C: Museum workers talk to visitors.
E: Visitors understand more about the objects.

C: You understand what the objects are.
E: You know more about the past.

C: You ask about the objects and pictures in your baby book. E: You know more about your history.

A New Country

Has your family ever moved to a new place? You might have been sad to leave because you would miss your friends. You might also have had to work hard to pack all your things so they got to your new home safely. But you might also have been excited because you would see new places.

A long time ago, many people decided to leave their homes. They wanted to live in the New World, which is what they called America before it became a country. These people had many reasons for wanting to travel far away from their homes.

Some of the people were called Pilgrims. They had a different religion, so the English government treated them badly. The Pilgrims wanted freedom to worship as they liked. They decided that they would have to leave England in order to have freedom.

Because they did not know much about the New World, the Pilgrims were nervous about leaving. But they got on ships and made the long journey anyway. When they got to the New World, they began their new lives.

The Pilgrims needed a lot of food to survive the cold winters. They went hunting so they could have meat like turkey, deer, and rabbit. They picked nuts and berries to store. Then, they would have food to eat during the long, cold months. They even learned how to plant corn so that they could pick it and eat it.

Native Americans showed the Pilgrims how to do all these things. Because the Native Americans had lived in the New World for a long time, they knew about all of these foods. They helped the Pilgrims, which made the Pilgrims grateful.

Later, many other people moved to the New World. Some people moved because they wanted to see new places. Some people moved because they needed to find good jobs. Some people moved because they did not like their old homes. After a while, so many people had moved to the New World that they decided to make their own country, called the United States.

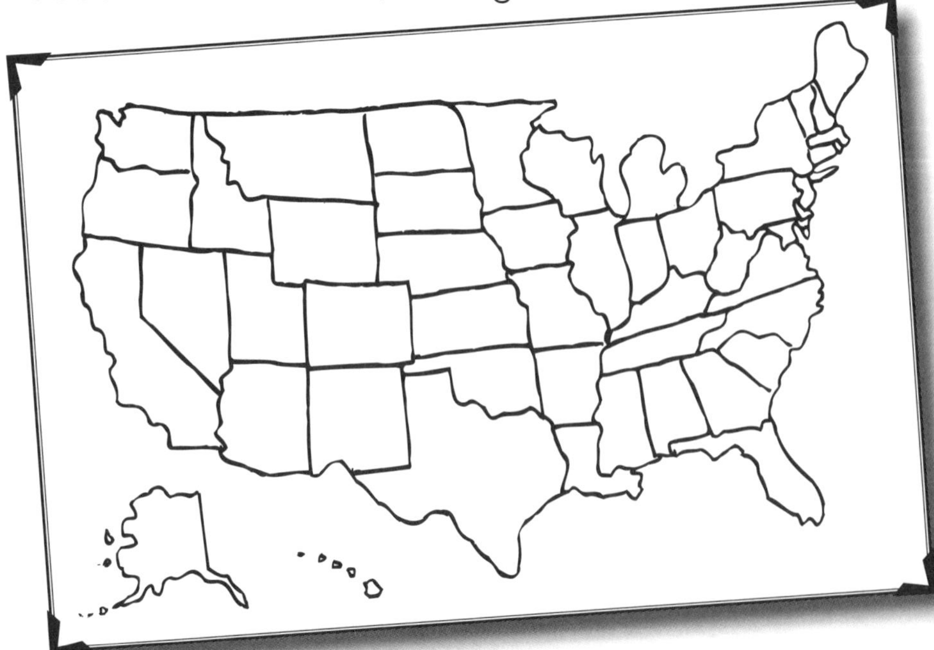

Learning about History

If you look at your baby book, you will see your own history. The person who took care of you pasted photos into the book. He or she wrote down important happenings. You can read about when you got your first tooth and what your first word was.

Your baby book shows what happened to you. It uses pictures and words to tell your story.

In the same way, history books show what happened to groups of people. Have you ever read about Pilgrims or pioneers? We know about these people from long ago because someone wrote down the things that happened. Someone else painted pictures, so we know what the world looked like back then.

Other people collected all those stories and pictures. They made them into history books. Because all of these people worked so hard, we can pick up books and learn all about the past.

But stories and pictures are not the only way to learn about the past. Look in your baby book again. Is there a little envelope filled with hair from your first haircut? Maybe there is a special card that someone sent you for your first birthday. These objects are part of your history, too. Someone saved a piece of your hair, so you can see and feel it. Someone saved that birthday card, so you can look at the signature.

Many old objects, such as coins and uniforms, are kept in museums. A museum is a place where people can learn about the past. Because a museum is open to the public, every person can go inside and see old objects.

At a museum, you can learn about different countries and the people who lived in them. You can also learn about the country where you live. Many teachers take their students on field trips to museums. Teachers want kids to see objects that they read about in history books.

Museum workers clean and take care of these old objects. They also talk to visitors about them. This helps the visitors understand more about the objects. When you understand what the objects are, you will know more about the past.

Look at your baby book again. Ask the person who took care of you to tell you about the objects. He or she can explain who the people in the pictures are. He or she can tell you stories about your past. Then you will understand more about your own history.

Cause-and-Effect Graphic Organizer

Name:____

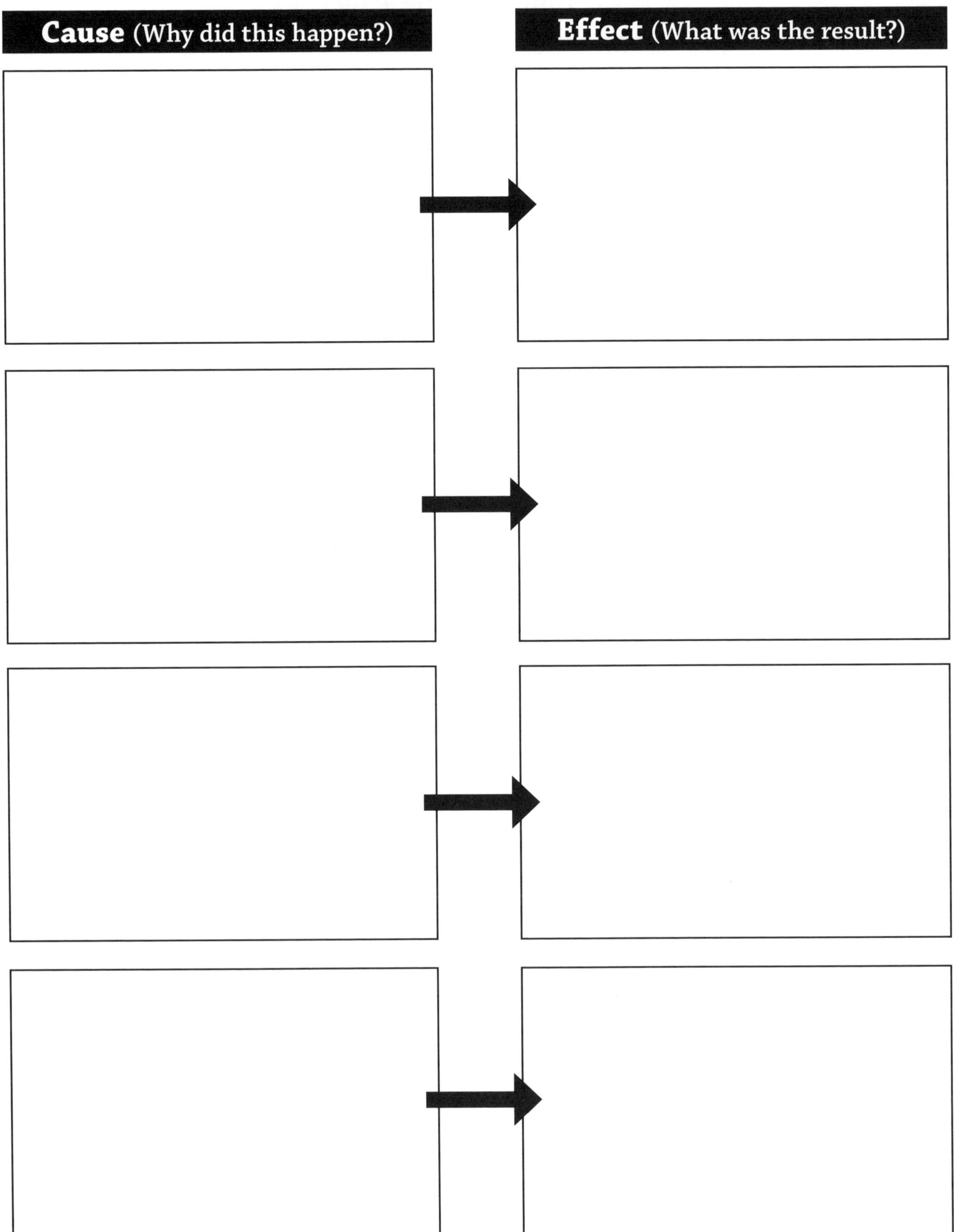

Directions: "Ready to Go" Story

Individual/Small Group ●/●●

Reproduce "Ready to Go" and "Ready to Go" Questions on pages 10 and 11 for each student. Have students read the story silently or aloud, answer the questions, and then discuss their answers with a partner.

Whole Class 

Reproduce the passage on a transparency and read it as a class. Divide the class into two teams. Have one player from each team come to the front of the room. Then, ask a question from the worksheet. The first player to answer correctly wins a point for his or her team. As an added challenge, ask students to identify other cause-and-effect examples in the story.

Answer Key

"Ready to Go" Questions (Page 11)

1. because her family was going on a trip to visit Grandma
2. so that Jack would not get out
3. she wants to leave on the trip right away
4. his face was covered with ice cream/everyone laughed/a little boy was upset
5. her dad tells her to/so that he will know what to do when they are gone
6. so he will remember what she says
7. he gets very thirsty
8. otherwise Jack will eat too much

Ready to Go

Anna got her suitcase with the pink flowers from the closet. Her family was going on a trip to visit Grandma. Anna packed some books. She also packed a game, a CD player, and a doll.

"Now I am ready to leave," thought Anna.

Anna walked down the stairs. She saw her dad taking suitcases to the car.

"Anna, please close the door for me," said Dad.

Anna closed the door. She did not want her dog, Jack, to run out. Sometimes Jack ran to another house. Jack liked to play with kids. He would beg them for something to eat.

One afternoon, Jack took an ice cream cone from a little boy. Jack's face ended up covered with ice cream. Everyone laughed at Jack. He looked so funny! The little boy was very upset, though. Anna promised to get another ice cream cone for him.

Anna did not want Jack to get out today. She wanted to leave on the trip right away.

Dad came back into the house with the neighbor boy, Sam. He would take care of Jack when Anna's family went on the trip.

"Anna," said Dad, "Please tell Sam about our dog."

First, Anna showed Sam where the dog bowls were.

"Keep the water bowl full," said Anna. "Jack gets so thirsty. He likes to drink lots of water."

Sam wrote a note about the water bowl on some paper.

"Feed Jack two times a day," said Anna. "Do not feed him more. He will eat too much!"

"I will feed Jack only twice a day," said Sam.

"After Jack finishes eating, he always goes outside," said Anna.

"Okay. I will remember to take Jack outside in the yard," said Sam.

"What else do you want to know?" asked Anna.

"I know what to do," said Sam. "I will take good care of Jack."

"Thanks, Sam!" said Anna.

"Ready to Go" Questions

Name:______________________

Directions: Read the story "Ready to Go." Then, answer the questions.

1. **Why did Anna pack her suitcase?**

2. **Why did Dad ask Anna to close the door?**

3. **Why does Anna want to be sure Jack doesn't get out today?**

4. **What happened in the past when Jack ate ice cream?**

5. **Why does Anna tell Sam how to take care of her dog?**

6. **Why is Sam writing notes while Anna is talking?**

7. **Why does Jack need lots of water in his bowl?**

8. **Why will Sam feed Jack his food only twice a day?**

Directions: Cause-and-Effect Signal Words

Individual ●

Reproduce Signal Words Fill-in-the-Blanks 1 and 2 on pages 13 and 14 for each student. Have the students fill in the blanks with the correct choices from the word bank. Explain that in some cases, more than one choice will fit in a blank. Remind students that it is important to reread each sentence with the selected choice to make sure the sentence makes sense.

Small Group ●●

Divide students into pairs or small groups. Reproduce Signal Words Fill-in-the-Blanks 1 or 2 for each student in the group. Have the students work together to fill in the blanks with the correct choices. Then, have students discuss the answer for each sentence. Encourage students to read the complete sentence when giving their answer. Often, students are more aware of the appropriateness of their answer when they hear it in context. Next, ask the students to discuss and label the parts of each sentence (cause or effect).

Whole Class ●●●

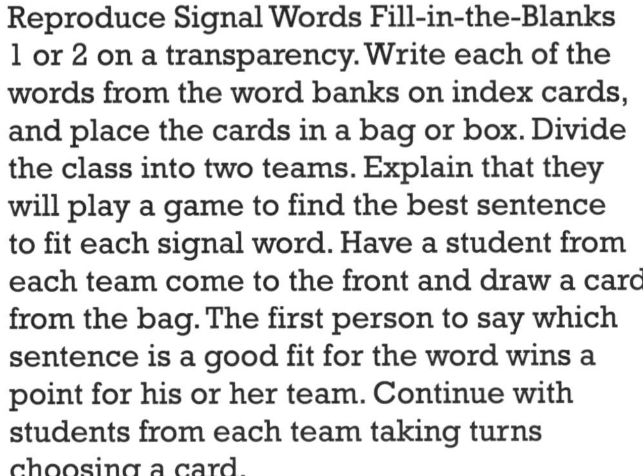

Reproduce Signal Words Fill-in-the-Blanks 1 or 2 on a transparency. Write each of the words from the word banks on index cards, and place the cards in a bag or box. Divide the class into two teams. Explain that they will play a game to find the best sentence to fit each signal word. Have a student from each team come to the front and draw a card from the bag. The first person to say which sentence is a good fit for the word wins a point for his or her team. Continue with students from each team taking turns choosing a card.

Game tip: Some students will find it easier to have a copy of the transparency as a worksheet they can follow on their own desk. This may be the case for students with visual tracking difficulties or low vision.

As an alternative game, ask students to state a cause-and-effect sentence aloud using the words they drew.

Answer Key

Signal Words Fill-in-the-Blanks 1 (Page 13)

1. so/therefore
2. since/because
3. Therefore/As a result
4. due to
5. since/because
6. The reason that
7. result
8. As a result/Therefore
9. cause
10. effect/result

Signal Words Fill-in-the-Blanks 2 (Page 14)

1. Therefore
2. because/since
3. since/because
4. the reason that
5. as a result of/due to
6. result/effect
7. so/therefore
8. cause
9. effect/result
10. in order to

Signal Words Fill-in-the-Blanks 1

Name:____________________

Directions: Choose the best word or words to finish each sentence. There can be more than one right answer.

1. The dress was too long, ____________________ my mother made it shorter.
2. Maria hasn't been able to ride her bike ____________________ she lost her helmet.
3. Only two games were left. ____________________ the shoppers hurried to get one.
4. It was hard to see ____________________ the mist that covered the trail.
5. The village honored the hero ____________________ he beat the enemy.
6. ____________________ the class earned money was to pay for the field trip.
7. Catching a cold was the ____________________ of not washing my hands.
8. The skunk lived in a hollow log. ____________________ it was safe from larger animals.
9. The matches were the ____________________ of the fire.
10. A flood was the ____________________ of many weeks of rain.

WORD BANK

therefore	result	so	cause	because
as a result	effect	since	due to	the reason that

Signal Words Fill-in-the-Blanks 2

Name:______________________

Directions: Choose the best word or words to finish each sentence. There can be more than one right answer.

1. The clown was doing some tricks. ______________________ a crowd gathered to watch what he was doing.

2. The milk was cold ______________________ it was kept in the refrigerator.

3. A nurse cared for the thin, old man ______________________ he was sick.

4. The holiday was ______________________ the people were joyful.

5. Jeff was unable to run with his friends ______________________ the cast on his leg.

6. The school has rules about running in the halls. The ______________________ is that the students walk in the halls.

7. A wind knocked the bottle on the deck, ______________________ it broke into many pieces.

8. The ______________________ of the flat tire was a nail.

9. A cat walked nearby. The ______________________ was the birds scattered.

10. My sister wore a wool jacket ______________________ keep warm.

WORD BANK

therefore	result	due to	cause	in order to	so
because	effect	since	as a result of	the reason that	

Directions: Finding Cause and Effect

Individual

Reproduce "The Fun Park" on page 16 or "A Tiny World" on page 17, along with the graphic organizer on page 18, for each student. Explain that students will read the story and then write sentences or draw pictures in the graphic organizer for the cause-and-effect examples they identify in the text. If students need additional space, instruct them to continue on the back of the graphic organizer.

Small Group

Divide the class into pairs. Reproduce "The Fun Park" or "A Tiny World" for each student, as well as a graphic organizer for each pair. Have the students take turns reading the story aloud. Then, have the students take turns identifying examples of cause and effect in the text. For example, if the first student finds an example of a cause, he or she should write or draw a picture that represents it in the graphic organizer. Then, the other student will write or draw the related effect. The activity continues until the graphic organizer is filled.

Whole Class 

Reproduce "The Fun Park" or "A Tiny World" for each student. Also, reproduce the graphic organizer on a transparency.

Have the students read the passage aloud with a partner. Then, split the students into two groups. One student will come to the overhead and write or draw either a cause or an effect from the text. Then, have a student from the other group write or draw the corresponding cause or effect. Continue in this manner until the graphic organizer is filled. Repeat with the second story. Then, discuss the activity as a class.

Answer Key (suggested answers)

"The Fun Park" (Page 16)

Cause: Jenna was going to the Fun Park.
Effect: She was happy.

Cause: Students got good grades.
Effect: The school gave them free tickets.

Cause: Jenna put on sunscreen.
Effect: She wouldn't get burned.

Cause: Jenna knew she would get hungry.
Effect: She packed a lunch.

Cause: She brought water.
Effect: She wouldn't get thirsty.

Cause: Jenna didn't want to miss the bus.
Effect: She ran to school.

Cause: The kids got bored on the bus.
Effect: They played games.

Cause: Jenna won the game.
Effect: She felt proud.

Cause: She looked at huge roller coasters.
Effect: She felt nervous.

Cause: She saw the other kids smile.
Effect: She felt better.

Cause: There were giant hills on the roller coaster.
Effect: Jenna's stomach flipped.

Cause: Jenna had fun on the Whizzer.
Effect: She rode it three more times.

Cause: Jenna was worn out from the fun day.
Effect: She fell asleep on the way home.

"A Tiny World" (Page 17)

Cause: Chad needed a jar for science class.
Effect: Chad asked his mother for a plastic snack jar.

Cause: Chad chose a plastic jar.
Effect: It would not break.

Cause: He washed and dried the jar.
Effect: It would be ready for his science project.

Cause: The class would be making terrariums.
Effect: They would show the water cycle on Earth.

Cause: Students put dirt and tiny plants in the jars.
Effect: The jars would be small models of Earth.

Cause: Students would add water to jars.
Effect: Evaporation would occur and plants would grow.

Cause: Water droplets would become heavy.
Effect: It would rain inside the jars and water the plants.

Cause: Too many water droplets collect in clouds.
Effect: It rains on Earth.

Cause: Students observe terrariums.
Effect: They learn about the water cycle.

The Fun Park

Jenna was very happy. Her class was going on a special field trip. They were going to the Fun Park. The school had given the students free tickets as a reward for getting good grades.

Jenna thought about all the things she needed to do for the day. She put on sunscreen so she wouldn't get burned. She knew she would get hungry, so she packed a lunch. She also brought water so she wouldn't get thirsty.

After she packed, Jenna ran the three blocks to school. She didn't want to miss the bus that was taking them to the park. She made it just in time to catch the bus.

On the long ride, the kids got bored. They played games to pass the time. Jenna was proud when she won the game by thinking of the most words that started with the letter "B."

Before they knew it, they were at the park. Jenna got nervous as she looked at the huge roller coasters. She heard kids screaming as they rode the coaster. She saw kids getting off the ride. After she saw the smiles on their faces, she felt better. They were having fun, and so would she.

Jenna decided to try the Whizzer first. The giant hills on the coaster made her stomach flip. She had so much fun that she rode the Whizzer three more times. Then, she rode as many other rides as she could before it was time to go home.

At the end of the day, Jenna sank into her seat on the bus. It was a great day. She'd had so much fun that she was worn out. She fell fast asleep on the way home.

A Tiny World

After dinner, Chad noticed that the giant snack jar was empty. He asked his mother if he could have it. He needed a plastic jar for his science project. Chad chose a plastic jar because it would not break. He washed and dried the jar so it would be ready for his science project.

Chad's teacher had told the class they would be making terrariums to show what happens during the water cycle on Earth.

First, the students would put dirt in the bottom of each jar. This would act like the soil on Earth. Then, they would place some tiny plants in the jars. The terrariums would become small models of Earth. Last, the students would add water to the jars to make the plants grow. The water would act like rain. Evaporation would cause water droplets to form on the top of the closed jars. When the water droplets became too heavy, it would rain inside the jars. This would show the students how rain worked on Earth. When too many water droplets collect in clouds, they fall to Earth as rain.

The "rain" in the jar would water the plants. Later, the water drops would collect at the top of the jar again. This would happen the same way water forms clouds in the sky.

By observing what happened in thier terrariums, Chad and his friends would learn about the water cycle. They would never even have to go outside to learn about the weather.

Science was so fun! Next, they were going to learn about simple machines. These were things like pulleys, levers, and wedges. Chad already knew these machines helped make work easier. He couldn't wait to find out how!

Cause-and-Effect Graphic Organizer

Name:____________________

Cause

Cause

Cause

Effect

Effect

Effect

Cause

Effect

Directions: Picture Match-Up

Individual ●

Reproduce multiple sets of the Picture Pair Cards on pages 20–23. Give several sets of cards to each student. Younger students or those who struggle with the concept of cause and effect might start with three or four pairs of cards. Other students might use 10 pairs.

Model matching the corresponding cause-and-effect pairs; then, have students try on their own. For an additional challenge, have students write a sentence for each picture pair.

Small Group ●●

Divide the class into pairs. Reproduce a complete set of Picture Pair Cards for each pair of students. Explain that they will play a memory match-up game. Spread the cards facedown on a table and have students take turns turning two cards over. If the cards are not a match, they must turn them facedown again. When a student gets a matching pair, he or she must identify the cause and the effect in order to keep the cards. The first student to get three matches wins the game.

Whole Group ●●●

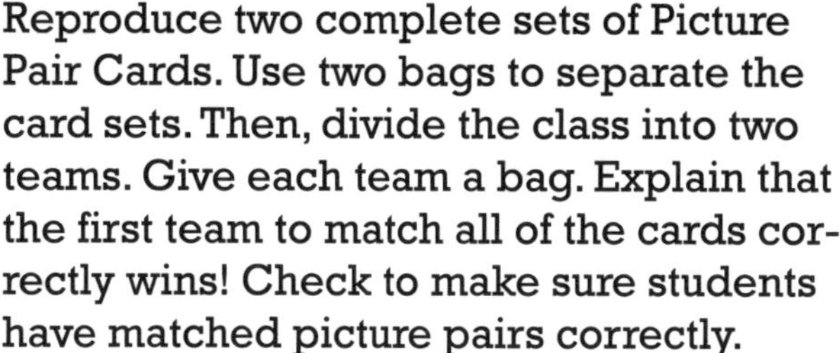

Reproduce two complete sets of Picture Pair Cards. Use two bags to separate the card sets. Then, divide the class into two teams. Give each team a bag. Explain that the first team to match all of the cards correctly wins! Check to make sure students have matched picture pairs correctly.

For an additional challenge, have the students write a sentence for each picture pair. If some students are struggling with writing cause-and-effect sentences, review possible signal or connecting words (so, because, since, as a result, the reason that, consequently, therefore, nevertheless, thus, due to the fact, the outcome was), and write them on the board for student reference as they are writing.

Picture Pair Cards 1

Picture Pair Cards 2

Picture Pair Cards 3

Picture Pair Cards 4

Directions: Cause and Effect Picture Clues

Individual/Small Group ●/●●

Reproduce Cause and Effect Picture Clues 1 or 2 on page 25 or 26 for each student. Explain that they will examine each picture and write what the corresponding cause or effect would be.

Whole Class 

Reproduce the pictures from Cause and Effect Picture Clues 1 and 2 on card stock or construction paper. Then, place the cards facedown on a table in the front of the room. Divide the class into two teams. Have one person from each team come to the front and choose a card. Students should not look at the card until you say, "Go." Then, each student writes a cause-and-effect sentence on the board based on the idea from the card. The first person to write a complete, accurate sentence wins a point for his or her team. Continue the game in this fashion as time allows or until a predetermined score has been reached.

Students who struggle with written language may need to give their sentence orally. You may also score the students simply on their ability to state the corresponding cause or effect.

Answer Key (suggested answers)

Cause and Effect Picture Clues 1 (Page 25)

1. Effect: The baby got food all over his face.
   Cause: The baby ate dinner.
2. Effect: She eats bowl of cereal.
   Cause: The girl was hungry.
3. Effect: He has to erase his answer.
   Cause: The boy made a mistake.
4. Cause: The baby reaches out to be picked up.
   Effect: The mother picks him up.
5. Cause: A boy gets a present.
   Effect: He opens it.
6. Cause: The woman takes cookies out of oven.
   Effect: She will serve freshly baked cookies.

Cause and Effect Picture Clues 2 (Page 26)

1. Effect: They receive a trophy.
   Cause: The kids won a game.
2. Effect: She makes a pair of mittens.
   Cause: A woman spent time knitting.
3. Effect: The soda spills.
   Cause: A kid knocked a soda over.
4. Cause: The man is setting up a tent.
   Effect: He will have a tent to sleep in.
5. Cause: A kid jumps into the pool.
   Effect: He makes a big splash.
6. Cause: The boy lets go of a balloon.
   Effect: The balloon floats away.

Cause and Effect Picture Clues 1

Name:______________________

Directions: Look at each picture. Write the missing cause or effect. For example, look at the baby with the messy face. How do you think he got messy?

Cause and Effect Picture Clues 2

Name:________________________

Directions: Look at each picture. Write the missing cause or effect. For example, look at the boy with the balloon. What is going to happen now that he let the balloon go?

Directions: Missing Cause or Effect

Individual

Reproduce Finish the Sentence 1 and 2 on pages 28 and 29 for each student. Explain that either the cause or the effect is provided. Tell students to fill in the blanks with the missing parts. Encourage them to read their complete sentences to make sure they have created logical sentences. Score based on sentence completeness and ability to understand the meaning.

Small Group

Pair students with partners, and give a different Finish the Sentence sheet to each student. Explain that this is a "think quick" activity. One student will read each sentence part on the first worksheet, and the other partner will finish the sentence. The "reader" will record the partner's answers. Then, have students switch roles with the new reader reading and filling in the second worksheet.

Whole Class 

Reproduce one of the Finish the Sentence worksheets on a transparency. Divide the class into two teams, and have one person from each team play each round. Show one sentence at a time on the overhead. The first person to yell out a needed cause or effect wins a team point. Silly sentences are encouraged!

Answer Key (suggested answers)

Finish the Sentence 1 (Page 28)

1. it was raining outside
2. Smoke was coming from the stove
3. We couldn't come in the house
4. it was her birthday
5. I got a bad grade
6. he asked his dad to pack one
7. he fixed it
8. I put on sunscreen

Finish the Sentence 2 (Page 29)

1. I had to stand
2. I stuck a pin in it
3. she watched it again and again
4. I couldn't stop reading it
5. it needs to reach leaves to eat
6. We had to go to bed
7. plants grew
8. The boat sank

Finish the Sentence 1

Name: ____________________

Directions: Read the sentences. Write a cause or an effect to finish each sentence.

1. The reason that I wore my rubber boots was that ____________________

____________________.

2. ____________________.
As a result, the smoke alarm went off.

3. ____________________ because
our feet were muddy.

4. The reason that Anna had a party was ____________________

____________________.

5. ____________________ because
I didn't hand in my homework.

6. Andy knew he had to bring a lunch, so ____________________

____________________.

7. The farmer saw a hole in the fence, so ____________________

____________________.

8. ____________________ because
I did not want a sunburn.

Finish the Sentence 2

Name:____________________

Directions: Read the sentences. Write a cause or an effect to finish each sentence.

1. All of the seats were taken, so ____.

2. The reason that the balloon popped was ____.

3. Since it was her favorite movie, ____.

4. Because the book was so exciting, ____.

5. The giraffe has a long neck because ____.

6. ____ since it was so late at night.

7. The students planted seeds in paper cups. The result was that ____.

8. ________________________ because there was a hole in it.

Directions: Using Graphic Organizers

Individual

Reproduce the Rain Cloud and Construction Graphic Organizers on pages 31 and 32 for each student. Review each graphic organizer with the students, explaining that *because* it is raining, there is a puddle on the ground; and *because* the hammer is pounding the nail, the nail is going into the wood. Using a book the class recently read, have each student fill in a cause with a related effect on each graphic organizer. Help students make the "rain = puddle" or "striking hammer = nail in board" connection with cause-and-effect relationships from their book. To help them find causes and effects, ask them why a character did something, or point to a picture and ask how an object got where it is. When all students have finished, hold a class discussion and invite students to share their graphic organizers with the class. How are the students' cause and effect examples alike or different?

Whole Class

Reproduce the Rain Cloud or Construction Graphic Organizer on a transparency. Explain that the class will use the graphic organizer to plan a story. Then, students will work together to create the story.

As a class, choose a topic for the story, such as "pets." Ask volunteers to give ideas to fill in the details of the graphic organizer. For example, Cause: Dogs need exercise. Effect: Therefore, they need to be walked. Repeat with more causes and effects. Use the extra lines to record the cause-and-effect examples the class comes up with.

Then, brainstorm to create a beginning sentence, or main idea, for the story. Write it on the board or a transparency. Then, have students take turns adding sentences to the story, including the cause-and-effect ideas the class came up with.

After the story is complete, have the group analyze it for cause-and-effect sentences. Use a blue marker to underline causes that were included in the story. Use a red marker to underline effects.

Alternate idea: Brainstorm for a topic and beginning sentence. Then, split the class into two groups. Have each group create a story. Then, as a class, evaluate the stories for cause-and-effect relationships. Compare stories: How are they similar? How are they different?

Note: These activities work best if the students are writing on a lined transparency, so that everyone will be able to see the story that is being discussed.

Rain Cloud Graphic Organizer

Name: ________________________

Cause

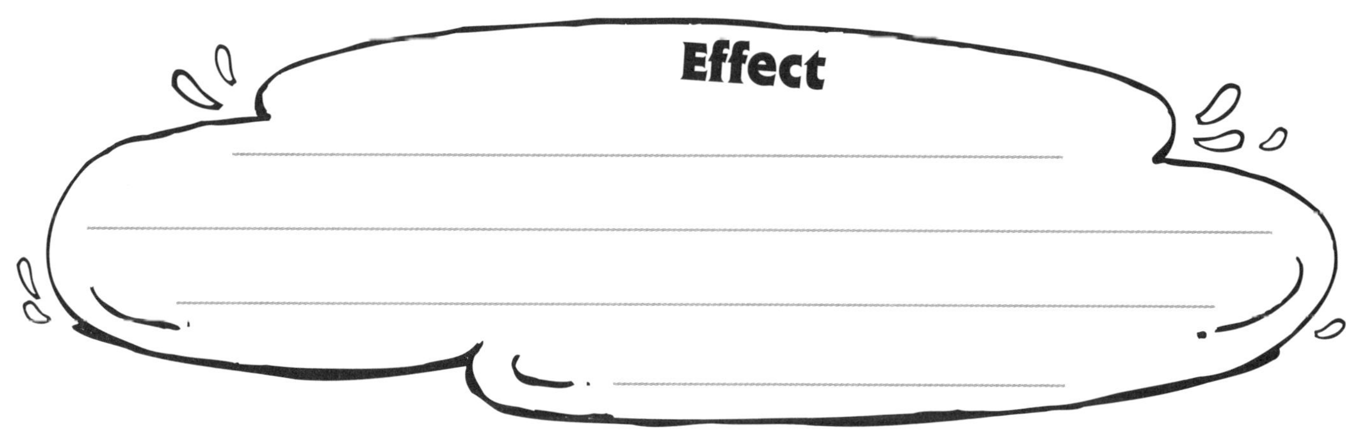

Construction Graphic Organizer

Name: ____________

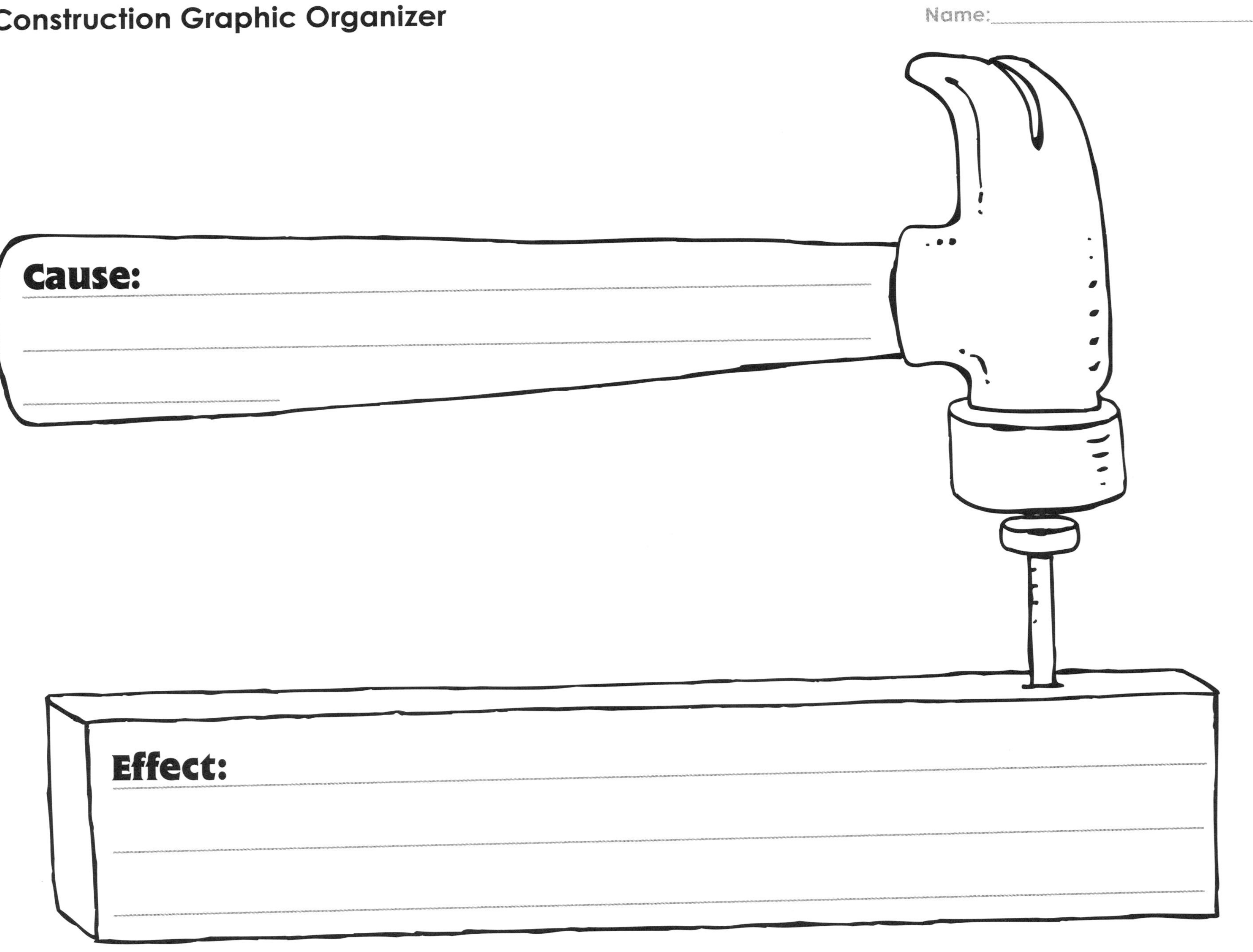

Directions: Adding Signal Words

Individual ●

Reproduce "The Clever Monkey" on page 34 and Putting "The Clever Monkey" In Order on page 35 for each student. Explain that "The Clever Monkey" sentences are mixed up, and that they will be putting them in order. First students will add cause-and-effect signal words from the word bank to each sentence or pair of sentences to make them into a cause-and-effect relationship. Remind students that signal words are words that let you know you're reading about a cause and effect. Review the words in the word bank together. Explain that more than one answer is possible. Then, have students write the sentences in the right order to create a story on the Putting "The Clever Monkey" In Order worksheet.

Small Group ●●

Divide students into small groups. Reproduce Putting "The Clever Monkey" in Order for each group. Using the sentences from the Individual activity, have students work together to put the sentences in order.

For further practice with signal words, reproduce the list of signal words on page 34 on a transparency and display for the students. Have them write a fill-in-the-blank sentence (with the signal word missing) for each. Then, have partners exchange sentences and fill in the missing words. Each student should also mark the cause (C) and effect (E) component of each sentence. Partners can compare and discuss their answers when they are finished.

Whole Class 

Reproduce the list of signal words on page 34 on a transparency and display for the students. Have each student write three sentences using the signal words. Divide the class into two teams. Have students from each team take turns reading one of their sentences. Is the sentence written correctly? If the other team can correctly identify the cause and the effect, that team wins a point. Play continues with teams alternating turns.

Answer Key

"The Clever Monkey," suggested answers (Page 34)

1. Finally
2. so
3. For this reason, As a result
4. because
5. As a result, Then
6. because
7. Then

Putting "The Clever Monkey" in Order (Page 35)

The family of monkeys had been taking a nap because they were tired from playing. But one monkey was very hungry. For this reason, he couldn't sleep. He wanted to find some food so his stomach would stop growling. He spied some bananas. He couldn't reach them because they were too high. Finally, he found a long stick he could use to get them down. He took a big swing at the plant. As a result, the bananas fell down on him. Then, the rest of the monkeys came running when they saw the feast the clever monkey had found.

The Clever Monkey

Name: ____________________

Directions: Use the words in the word bank to make the sentences into cause-and-effect sentences. Write the words in the blanks. Words can be used more than once.

1. ____________, he found a long stick he could use to get them down.

2. He wanted to find some food ____________ his stomach would stop growling.

3. But one monkey was very hungry. ____________ he couldn't sleep.

4. He spied some bananas. He couldn't reach them ____________ they were too high.

5. He took a big swing at the plant. ____________, the bananas fell down on him.

6. The family of monkeys had been taking a nap ____________ they were tired from playing.

7. ____________, the rest of the monkeys came running when they saw the feast the clever monkey had found.

Word Bank

so
because
As a result
Finally
For this reason
Then

Putting "The Clever Monkey" in Order

Name:

Directions: Use the cause-and-effect sentences you wrote to put the story in order. Think about what might have happened first, second, third, etc.

The Clever Monkey

Directions: "Sweet Lemons" Story

Individual ●

Reproduce "Sweet Lemons" and the "Sweet Lemons" Recording Sheet on pages 37 and 38. Explain that the students should read the story for understanding, watching for examples of cause and effect. Then, students should use the recording page to list the cause-and-effect ideas present in the story.

Small Group ●●

Divide the class into small groups. Reproduce "Sweet Lemons" and the corresponding recording sheet for each group. Have the small groups read the story together, taking turns reading aloud. Then, as a group, they should record the cause-and-effect examples from the story on the sheet. Finally, have each group share and discuss their findings with the class. Compare different groups' findings.

Whole Class ●●●

Reproduce "Sweet Lemons" on a transparency. Also, reproduce one recording sheet for each student. Tell students they should listen for cause-and-effect examples. Read the story aloud. After the entire story has been read, remove the transparency, and give the students one minute to record as many cause-and-effect pairings from the story as they can remember. Students will share answers with the class and discuss accuracy. The student with the most accurate answers wins a classroom reward (free time, extra recess, silent reading, a beanbag chair to use for the day, etc.).

Answer Key (suggested answers)

"Sweet Lemons" Recording Sheet (Page 38)

Cause: School was out for the summer. Effect: Josh and Amy could do fun things all day long.

Cause: Mrs. Johnson wanted to invite Josh and Amy to the pool. Effect: She called their mother.

Cause: Josh and Amy would be able to see their friends and cool off at the pool.
Effect: They were very excited.

Cause: Mrs. Johnson needed to go home to fix supper. Effect: They packed up to leave the pool.

Cause: Josh and Amy could not come to the pool everyday. Effect: They felt sad.

Cause: Mrs. Johnson wanted to tell their mother how nicely Josh and Amy acted.
Effect: She called their mother.

Cause: Going to the pool was fun. Effect: They wanted to go every day.

Cause: They did not have enough money. Effect: They could not get a pool pass.

Cause: They will make money from the lemonade stand.
Effect: They will be able to buy a pool pass.

Cause: They got a table and chairs. Effect: Their stand would be like a real business.

Cause: They made a sign. Effect: People would know the cost of the lemonade.

Cause: They saved money. Effect: They had enough money to buy a pool pass.

Cause: Josh gave money to the man behind the desk. Effect: He gave them pool passes.

Cause: They handed their passes to the girl at the gate. Effect: She let them inside.

Sweet Lemons

School was out for the summer. That meant Josh and Amy could do fun things all day long. They loved going to the park. They loved playing games with their friends. They loved taking their dog, Lucky, for walks.

One afternoon, Mrs. Johnson called their mother. She wanted to invite Josh and Amy to go to the swimming pool. She explained to their mother that she went with her own children to the pool every day.

"Sweet," said Josh when Mom told them about the invitation.

Josh and Amy were very excited about going to the pool. They would be able to see many of their friends. They would also be able to cool off from the hot summer temperatures.

The afternoon at the pool was as wonderful as they hoped. Too soon, it was four o'clock, and Mrs. Johnson needed to go home to fix supper. They packed up to leave. Josh and Amy felt a little sad. They would not be able to come to the pool every day like so many of their friends.

That evening, Mrs. Johnson called Mom again. She wanted to tell Mom how nicely Josh and Amy had acted at the pool.

Then, Mrs. Johnson said something else. She explained that Josh and Amy could buy a summer pass and go to the pool every day.

Going to the pool was fun. Josh and Amy liked the idea of going every day. They only had one problem. A pool pass cost money. They could not get one because they didn't have enough money.

The next afternoon, Amy had an idea.

"Let's have a lemonade stand," she said to Josh. "We'll make money. Then, we can buy a pass for the pool."

"Sweet," said Josh.

Josh and Amy got a table and chairs. Their lemonade stand would look like a real business. They got water, sugar, and lemons. The lemonade would taste great. They made a sign so people would know the cost of the lemonade.

Every day for a week, Josh and Amy sold lemonade. They saved the money so they could each buy a pool pass.

Finally, they had enough money to buy the passes, and they went to the pool with Mom.

Josh handed the money to the man behind the desk. The man handed him back two passes.

Josh and Amy remembered the lemonade stand work. They looked at each other and smiled.

"Sweet!" they both said.

The next day, Josh and Amy went to the pool with the Johnsons. They handed their passes to the girl at the gate, and she let them inside for a cool, fun afternoon.

"Sweet Lemons" Recording Sheet

Name:

Directions: Read "Sweet Lemons." Then, write all of the cause-and-effect examples from the story on the lines below.

• CAUSE •	• EFFECT •

Directions: Cause-and-Effect Story Starters

Whole Class 

Introduce the activity by reading a book that exemplifies cause and effect, such as one of Laura Joffe Numeroff's books, including *If You Give a Mouse a Cookie*, *If You Give a Moose a Muffin*, or *If You Give a Pig a Pancake*. Discuss the examples of cause and effect throughout the story.

Individual/Small Group 

Reproduce Cause-and-Effect Stories on page 40 for each student. Have each student choose an idea from the list. They should write their own cause-and-effect story in the style of the story read as a class. This is a time for students to summarize their understanding of cause and effect into their own writing. The stories they write may be silly or serious. Then, have students work in pairs. They should share their stories with each other, labeling all of the cause-and-effect examples they can find. Then, invite volunteers to share their stories with the rest of the class.

Check to make sure students have included examples of cause and effect in their stories. Monitor partner work to make sure they are correctly identifying cause-and-effect pairs. At the end of the activity, put all of the stories in a binder to create a class book.

Cause-and-Effect Stories

Name:

Directions: Think about the cause-and-effect story that you read with your class. Then, choose one of the story starters below, or think of your own. Write your story on the lines. Draw one example of cause and effect from your story in the circles.

- If you give me an apple . . .
- If you give a frog a diving board . . .
- If you give my sister/brother a tightrope . . .
- If you give a cat a noodle . . .
- If you give my class bubble gum . . .
- If you give my mom a basketball . . .

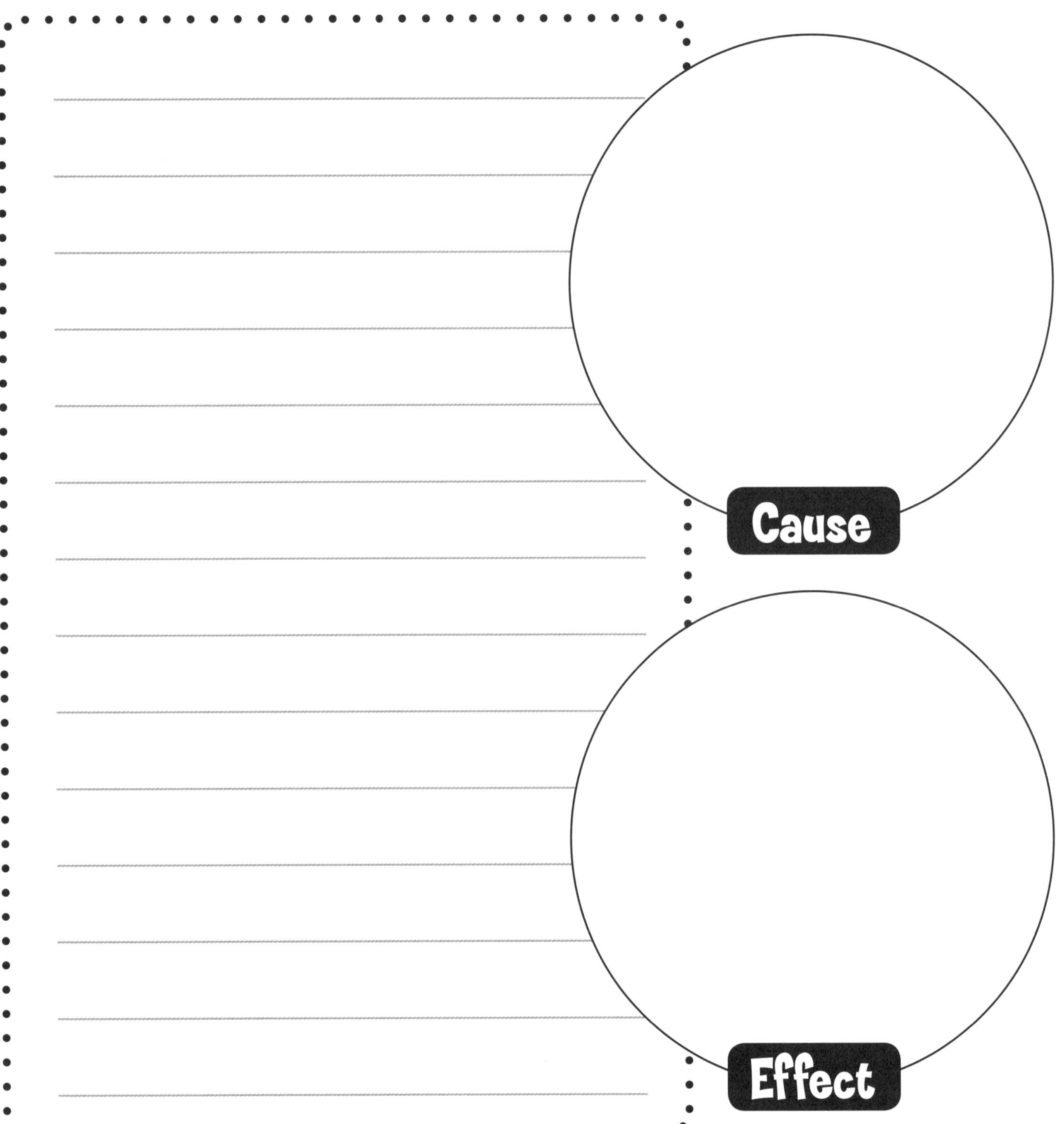

Directions: Cause and Effect with Science

Individual ●

Reproduce either "Trick or Treat" or "Waiting for Spring" and their corresponding question sheets on pages 42–45 for each student. Explain that each student should read the passage, paying special attention to cause-and-effect relationships; then, answer the questions. You may also wish to have the students mark each cause and effect by underlining the cause and circling the effect, or drawing an arrow from the cause to the effect. When all students have finished, go over the worksheets as a class.

Small Group/Whole Class ●●/●●●

Complete the passage and question activity for individuals. Then, split the class into groups of three or four students. Have the students brainstorm other cause-and-effect examples from nature. Allow the groups time to research on the Internet or with other resource materials. Provide each group with materials to create a poster illustrating one cause-and-effect relationship they learned about. Have each group present their poster to the class.

Answer Key

"Trick or Treat?" Questions (Page 43)

1. Animals use camouflage to hide from other animals.
2. Many animals are white so they can hide in snow.
3. Some turtles are green so they can hide in plants.
4. Shape can help by making the insect look like other things.
5. Some markings help by making animals look like other things.

"Waiting for Spring" Questions (Page 45)

1. Bears hibernate because there is little food in the winter.
2. Cold can cause animals to hibernate to keep warm.
3. Animals in the desert stay cool by burying themselves in sand.
4. Hornets add paper to their nests so that they will be warm in the winter.
5. Heat can make some animals hibernate to keep cool.

Trick or Treat?

Animals have dangerous lives. This is because other animals may want to eat them. Sometimes animals can hide so they don't get eaten. They might have the same color as things around them. They might also have the same markings or the same shape. This is called camouflage.

Camouflage can be color. Many animals and insects have the same coloring as their habitat. Color can make them hard to see. They can stay safe from animals or insects. Polar bears and snowshoe rabbits are white. Because of this, other animals can't see them against the white snow. A turtle can be green so it can hide in green plants. Another example is a walking stick. They are brown. Twigs are brown, too. In fact, you might even think a walking stick was a twig if you saw one!

Camouflage can be markings, too. Zebra's stripes are markings. The stripes look like the tall grass that zebras live near. It is hard to see the zebras against the grass. This makes it hard for lions to see them and eat them.

Some creatures also have the shape of things where they live. An example is the walking stick. It has the color of a stick. It also has the shape of a stick. This makes it hard to see.

Sometimes a moth can look like another animal. The markings on its wings look like giant eyes. The big eyes can make other animals think the moth is a large animal. This will scare them away. Markings can keep the moth safe.

The world of camouflage is interesting. Colors, markings, and shape are important to stay safe. Camouflage helps animals and insects hide. If they don't trick the other animals, they might end up being their treat!

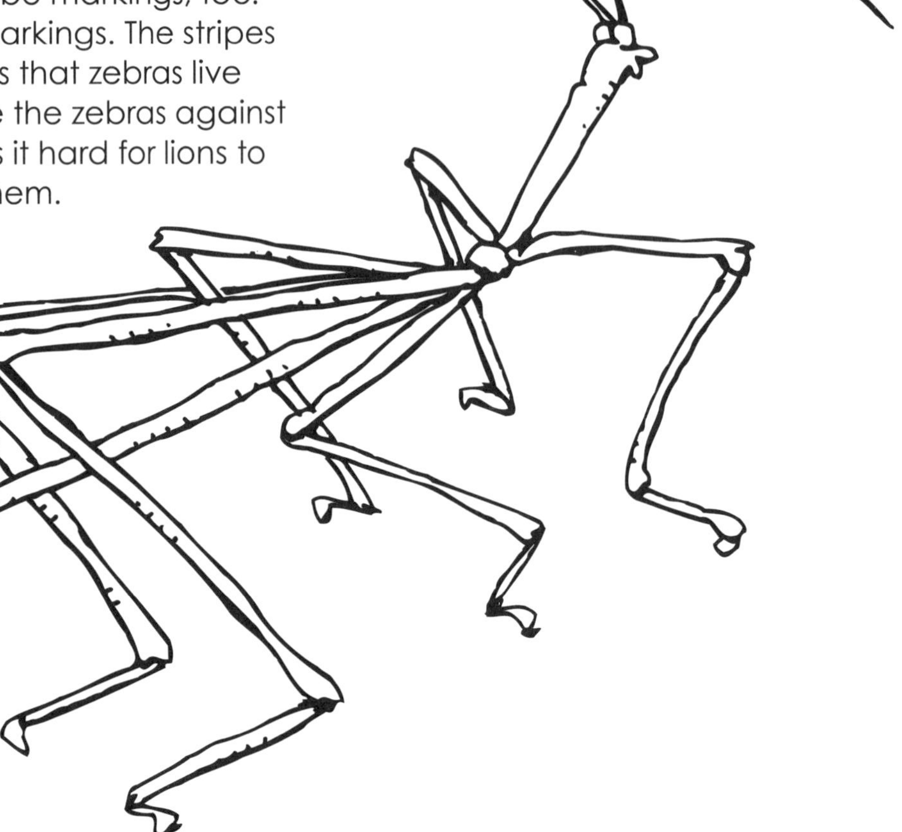

"Trick or Treat?" Questions

Name:

1. Why do animals use camouflage?

2. Why are many animals white?

3. Why are some turtles green?

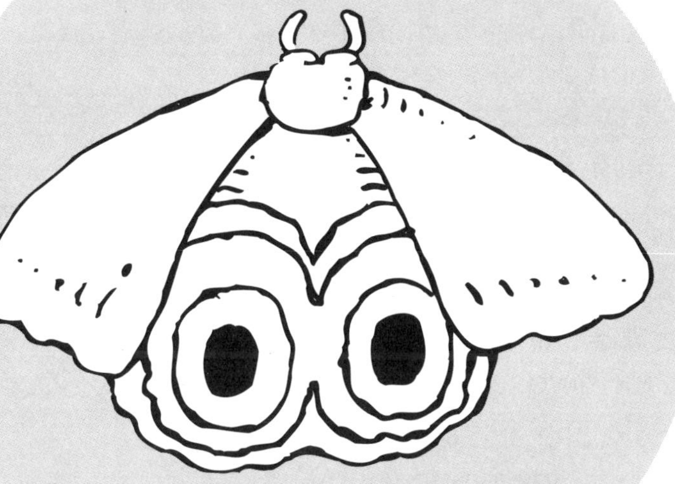

4. How does an insect's shape keep it safe?

5. How do marks help some animals?

Waiting for Spring

In spring and summer, most animals move a lot. In fall, they are active, too. Winter can be very different. It is a time when many animals hibernate. Some animals that hibernate are bears, bats, fish, and chipmunks. Squirrels, skunks, opossums, and frogs can hibernate, too. Even some insects hibernate. Hornets are examples of insects that hibernate.

What is hibernation? It is a time when an animal slows down. Its heart rate slows down. Its breathing slows down. Its body temperature is lower. This helps protect the animal in winter when there is not as much food and it is very cold.

Because there is not much food, hibernation helps the animals. While they sleep, they don't use much energy. They can live off their body fat. They also use some food that they saved. The animals can wait until spring for more food.

In the winter, the temperature is cold. Slowing down to hibernate keeps the animal warm. Some frogs live in outside ponds. These animals slow down, too. They stay in a place that is safe. They do not move much until spring. In the spring, it will be warmer. Then, they will move more.

Hornets live in paper nests. All summer, the hornets add to the walls of the nest. By the winter, the walls of the nest are thick. The nest keeps the hornets warm until spring. Then, they move around more.

Hibernation does not always happen in the winter. Sometimes it happens in the summer. This is true for some animals that live in the desert. The temperatures are too hot for them to live. They might wait out the heat by burying themselves in the sand. This is because it is a little cooler than in the hot sun.

Hibernation is not just going to sleep. It is changing the body's way of doing things. It is nature's way of keeping the animals safe until spring.

"Waiting for Spring" Questions

Name:

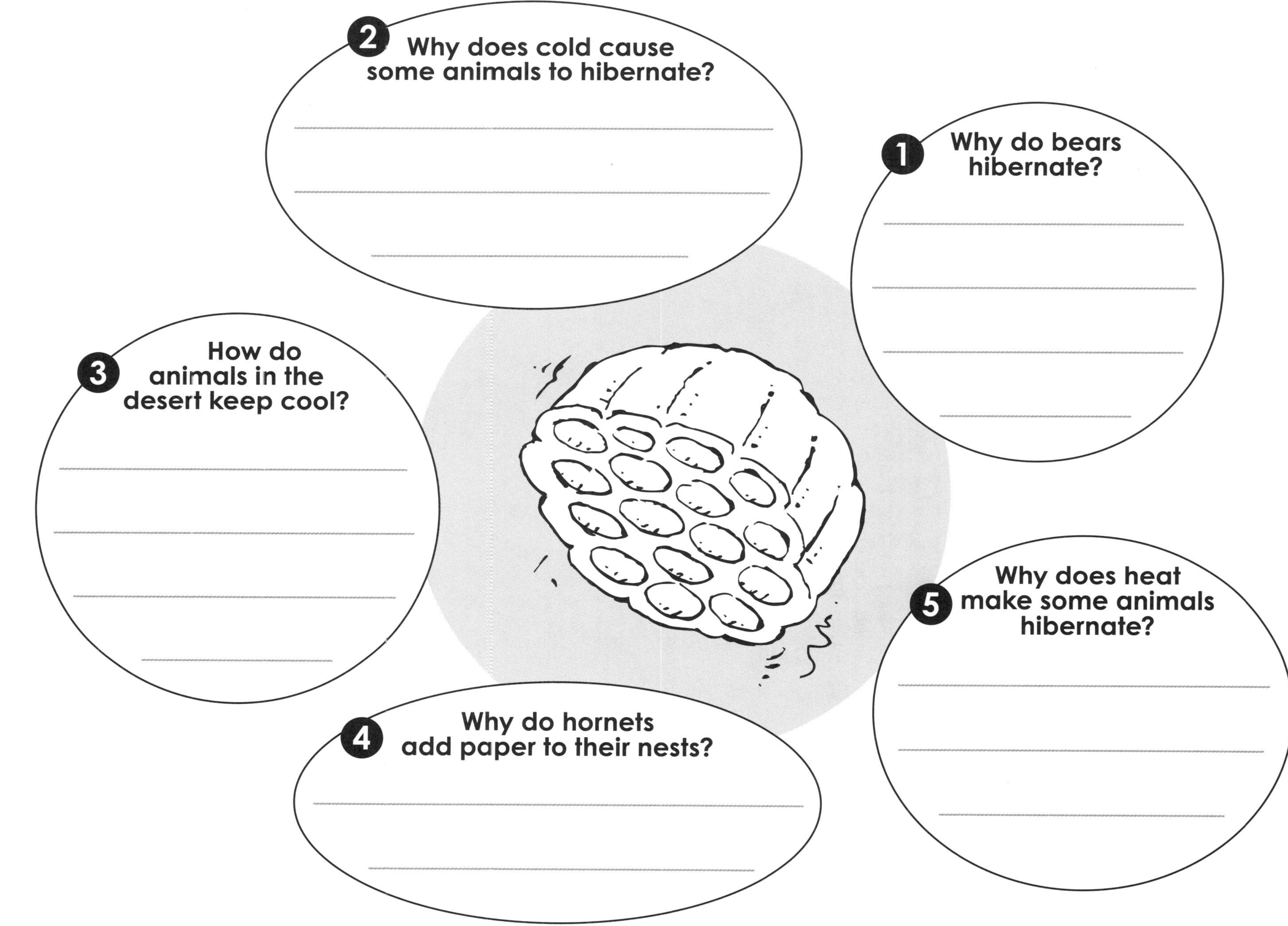

Directions: Think Quick! Games

Small Group ●●

Play a game with Think Quick! Cards 1 and 2 on pages 47 and 48. Reproduce a set of cards for each group of four students. Place the cards facedown in the middle of the group. Students take turns drawing a card and reading it to the group. The first person to come up with an ending for the sentence wins a point. Continue in this manner with one student serving as the scorekeeper.

Small Group/Whole Class 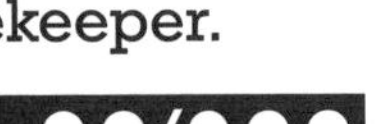

Get students out of their seats for this Think Quick! game. You will need a set of game cards, a bag, and a soft ball. Reproduce the Think Quick! Cards on card stock or other heavy paper. Cut the cards apart, and place them in a bag. Give the ball to the first student. Draw a card, and read it aloud. The student holding the ball quickly tosses the ball to another person in the circle. That person must complete the sentence. Then, read aloud a new card. The student with the ball quickly tosses it to another student. The game continues in this manner until all students have had a turn.

Challenge students to come up with two or three Think Quick! Cards to add to the game.

Ethan needed one more dime
to buy the candy, so...

The children studied the map
at the zoo because...

A mailman carries a bag so that...

It had been raining
all morning. As a result,...

The little boy blamed his
sister for the fall since...

The box was filled with
heavy books. Therefore,...

All the students were
overjoyed because of...

The frog jumped into
the pond. As a result,...

I had to go to bed early because...

The batter swung as hard as he could. The result was...

Evan had to pack for camp, so he...

Because it was so windy...

Rosa made a funny face because...

His mother moved the toys so that...

Many animals in the arctic are white because...

The baby was upset when his mother left. As a result,...

It was difficult to catch the butterfly, due to the fact that...

Because the team scored the winning goal, the crowd...